# PRAYERS FROM THE HEART

# Prayers from the Heart

## A COLLECTION OF 77 PRAYERS BY TOPIC

Loretta Fralin-Rapp

Lilyeve Publishing

First Printing, 2024

I would like to dedicate this book of prayers to my daughter, Danielle. From the moment I met you and got to be your mom, I knew I was given someone special. Your tender heart, sensitivity and love toward others at such a young age, was a blessing to me. And even though we aren't together and don't get to have a traditional relationship, you are always in my heart. The way in which our lives have been pulled apart has left me broken, yet clinging to the God that I hope you will encounter. These prayers come out of place of relationship with God who has sustained me through the many years of our separation and has walked with me for 40 years. I want you to know God loves you even more than I do and He's waiting for you to talk to Him just like you talk to a best friend. He can change your life. I know He's changed mine. I love you, sweetheart!

# *Acknowledgements*

I am very grateful for my good friend Ben Yoder, who was a constant source of support as I wrote these prayers. There were many times where we had conversations over FaceTime and prayed together just to help me work through some difficult moments, especially as I prepared to write the Abandonment Prayer and the Trust Prayer. He has been instrumental in helping me to see this project through to completion. I also want to thank my friend Janis Pomeroy, who supported me in prayer, especially as I wrote the Motherhood Prayer. That was an important moment, and she held my hand and spoke loving words over me and for that I am thankful. I am blessed to have these two!

# Contents

## 2
# Relationships                              63

**4**
# Practices                                    **189**

# *Introduction*

Hello dear reader! As you pick up this book of prayers, I want you to know that this work feels like the culmination of 40 years of relationship with God and there are many prayers here that exist because of a genuine desire to know God and to experience all that He has for me. The idea for this prayer book actually developed after I started working on Prayers from the Heart, a meditation that I decided to put together last year. You see, I have bipolar disorder and last year I went through one of the darkest depressions I had ever experienced. While I was in outpatient treatment, the counselor talked about coping strategies and she listed several things like prayer, meditation, creativity, music and many others, but these got my attention. I thought, maybe I can come up with a meditation video of a collection of prayers that I can listen to when I am struggling with depression, because I knew the day would come again. It's part of the disorder.

So, I decided to create a meditation video with me reading the prayers and I used my nature photography as the focal point, along with relaxing music by Kevin MacLeod. The videos are powerful, and they are relaxing. I decided to make them free on YouTube and you can find all four videos under Prayers from the Heart (parts 1-4). While I was making the videos I decided to put together the prayer book so that listeners could follow along if they desired to, or just have access to the prayers whenever they wanted. The book has an interaction section where you can write your own prayers and then write down God's response as He speaks to you. This prayer book is great to use on a silent retreat and the videos are great to listen to before bedtime or if you're up in the middle of the night and struggle to sleep, as I do sometimes. I've already used the videos a few times in the middle of the night, and it soothed me like a warm blanket and helped me get back to sleep after I found myself agreeing with the prayers as I heard them.

The prayer book is broken up into four sections, Qualities to Embrace, Relationships, Challenges to Overcome and Practices. While the list of prayers is not exhaustive, there are 77 prayers and the topics covered are ones like Peace, Love, Depression, Loneliness, Faith, Trust, Abandonment and Acceptance. These prayers are intimate and meaningful to me, and I hope you will find in these prayers a way to start some conversations with God that will open the door to a walk with Him you never knew you could have. He's waiting for you!

Blessings,
Loretta Fralin-Rapp

# 1

# Qualities to Embrace

# 1

## Beauty

**Isaiah 61:3**

# Beauty Prayer

Father,

Your word promises that you will give beauty for ashes, joy instead of mourning and praise instead of despair. I am desperate to receive these things. I've experienced so many hard things and I carry around the ashes and the heavy burden of those experiences. I want to give you my ashes and trust that you will exchange them for beauty, but honestly, I don't know what beauty would look like. I want it. I want to experience beauty in my life, love in my life and hope for a good and better future. Lord, would you show me beauty as you see it? Help me to see the beauty around me that already exists. Give me eyes to see beauty in your creation, beauty in a meaningful conversation, beauty in the laughter of a child, beauty in the expression of love. I desire to experience beautiful love with you that lifts me out of despair and mourning and sets me on a rock that is high above my circumstances so I can see Jesus, the One who gave it all for me. His sacrifice is truly beautiful because it's restored me to a right relationship with you. I want to know you more and to walk in the beauty that exists in your presence. I surrender my heart to you Lord. Transform me so that I reflect your beauty.

In Jesus' Name,
Amen

# Interaction

Your Prayer:

God's Response:

# 2

# Contentment

Philippians 4:11-13

# Contentment Prayer

Father,

I believe that the secret to contentment is to receive everything I need from you and to believe that if you mean for me to have something, you will provide it. But I also know that you tell me to ask for what I need, so I can't be content if I'm not willing to ask you for what I need. I realize it's important for me to do my part and trust that you will do yours. When I do this, I can be satisfied with what is within my power to do and I can rest and be secure in who you are in my life and in what you have made available to me. You provide me with everything I need, and I am grateful for that. Lord, continue to grow in me an understanding of what it means to be content and help me to walk in contentment and trust that you will always be with me and that in your presence, I am complete, whole, and fully satisfied.

In Jesus' Name,

Amen

## Interaction:

Your Prayer:

God's Response:

# 3

# Encouragement

**Jude 1:20**

# Encouragement Prayer

Father,

I need your encouragement today. I find myself discouraged by the things that haven't turned out in my life the way I thought they would. Help me to let go of the idea I have in my head of the perfect life and instead choose the life you want for me. Encourage my heart and build hope in me for the better life I get to have with you. God, I'm lonely and sometimes that hurts more than anything, but I know that if I use what you've given me, the ability to pray in the Spirit, I will experience your encouragement as well as an answer to my deepest longings. Help me to be intentional about taking time to use my prayer language and pray in the Spirit. Help me to experience you in worship and become solid in my understanding of what can happen when you show up in my life. When you show up mountains move, when you show up bondages are broken, when you show up peace rests on my heart, when you show up, I am forever changed. Show up in my life today and build up the kind of courage in me that leads me to face my giants and live on purpose.

In Jesus' Name,
Amen

## Interaction

Your Prayer:

God's Response:

# 4

# Faith

Hebrews 11:1
Mark 11:22-24

# Faith Prayer

Father,

I love how the Passion translation defines faith. "Faith brings our hopes into reality and becomes the foundation needed to acquire the things we long for." You know my heart longs for many things. There are desires in my heart that I believe you put there, and I want to have the faith to believe that you will meet me in my longing and grant those desires. I want to live with your kind of faith and believe that what I ask for will happen. Grant me great faith to see mountains moved, the path made clear and to have the confidence to walk in the destiny you've created for me. Help me to always come to you in prayer, believe that you are listening and ask for what's in my heart. I want to believe you will grant my requests, but sometimes I've heard you say no so it's shaken my faith to ask again. Help me to ask for things that are in line with your will for me and help me to always be true to my heart. Help my unbelief when circumstances seem impossible. Let your faith rise in me until I walk with your confidence and speak with your determination and certainty.

In Jesus' Name,

Amen

# Interaction

Your Prayer:

God's Response:

# 5

# Gentleness

**Colossians 3:12**

# Gentleness Prayer

Father,

My ability to be gentle and humble comes from you alone. It's because of your transforming love that I can find the strength within me to extend mercy to others. I want to walk around with the glasses of mercy, that make me unoffendable, because I see who's really behind that behavior. When I see with these glasses, compassion and kindness come easier, because when I look at the one who seeks to harm me, I see myself and my own weaknesses and how the enemy has used me to harm others. In that moment of clear vision, I find forgiveness for myself and for others. Thank you for choosing me to be holy, set apart for special use, and for giving me the desire to want to understand others instead of being quick to blame and judge their intentions as harmful. Grant me the grace to be gentle as I approach the ones who are hurting and are only acting out of their own brokenness. Let my words be seasoned with love that comes from an understanding heart. When I care for the one with the thorn in his paw, keep me humble, patient and always reaching out with gentleness as I touch their heart and soothe their soul.

In Jesus' Name,

Amen

## Interaction

Your Prayer:

God's Response:

# 6

## God's Timing

### Habakkuk 2:3

# God's Timing Prayer

Father,

It's so important to trust your timing. If I try to get out ahead of you and make things happen on my own, I'll birth things that will be detrimental to the blessings you've prepared for me. I don't want to create more problems for myself by not waiting for you to fulfill the promises you've made to me. You give me vision and you give me your word to hold onto, let that be enough to sustain me as I hold onto the faith you've placed inside me. When I begin to become impatient, would you use a trusted friend to speak words of encouragement to me that build my hope for what you are doing in my life? I know that sometimes I need help to wait because I lose perspective when the promise seems so far away. Give me a strategy in the waiting, so that I hold on tightly to your promise but loosely to how that promise will look when it's fulfilled. Help me to see the blessing when it arrives and thank you for it. When you're working things out for my good, help me to catch a glimpse of that work and know that what I hope for is coming and it will not be delayed.

In Jesus' Name,
Amen

# Interaction


Your Prayer:






God's Response:

# 7

# God's Will

### Matthew 6:9-13

# God's Will Prayer

Father,

Jesus taught us to pray that your kingdom come, and your will be done here on earth. I know sometimes I fight against your will, because I want to have my own way, but really if I submit to your will in my life, I will find a better experience than I could have dreamed of for myself. Help me to see your will, desire, and purpose as more important and not be so selfish with my life. There's work to be done and lives that need to be saved and it's time for me to be about your business and stop getting so caught up in how to meet my own needs. You are good and you provide for me, so why do lose sight of that, and think I have to make things happen on my own? You tell me that if I seek first your kingdom, everything else I need will be provided. Help me to live like I believe that and stay focused on the things you've given me to do on this earth. May your kingdom purpose be accomplished in my life, both now and in eternity.

In Jesus' Name,

Amen

# Interaction

Your Prayer:

God's Response:

# 8

## Grace

**Hebrews 4:14-16**

# Grace Prayer

Father,

Sometimes I am so weak. I give into temptation and that creates so many problems in my life. I'm so grateful that Jesus, as my King and Priest, understands my frailties and sympathizes with me. He doesn't condemn me and neither do you. He makes intercession for me, so I can come to this incredible throne of grace with boldness instead of in fear and insecurity. Here I find the grace I desperately need, as well as your mercy. I need your grace to help me when I'm struggling, and I feel all alone. I need your grace to strengthen me when my mind waivers and depression is easier to settle into than faith. When I'm at that crossroads of depression and faith, would you release your grace to me in that moment and shine a light on the path that leads to faith, so that I come closer to you instead of sinking into despair. Thank you for the power in your grace. You tell me that your grace is more than enough for me and that your power finds its full expression through my weakness. So, in my weakness I get to experience your power flowing through me and I get to be a witness who can share that experience with others. My weakness creates an opportunity for your power to be seen, so I choose to embrace that truth and to no longer be down on myself when I'm feeling weak. Instead, I will call on you to help me and empower me to do the very thing I never thought I could do. Help me to stand with you and stand for you today and to embrace the grace you offer.

In Jesus' Name,
Amen

## Interaction

Your Prayer:

God's Response:

# 9

# Happiness

**Psalm 146:5**

# Happiness Prayer

Father,

Your word says that happiness comes from putting my hope in you. I want to believe that. Happiness is something that has been elusive for me and the few moments where I've found it, it goes away just as quickly as it came. I desire to be happy in this life and I believe you want that for me as well. In those moments where I struggle to hope in you, would you come close to me and speak words that breathe life and that lead to happiness. May the revelation from you open my eyes to see the joy that is in front of me. Help me to see my life through your eyes, because when I do, I'm sure my outlook will be so different. I want a perspective that causes me to cling to you, not because I'm afraid, but because I'm so drawn to the love and peace that come from you. I think if I could settle in there, I would experience so much more happiness in my life. It has to come from you first and I have complete access to you, so what am I waiting for? I think sometimes my pride gets in the way. I feel like I should be able to find happiness on my own and when I try, the darker it gets. You are my light and my life and when I'm with you, I feel most like myself. Help me not to fight against your process, but instead to go with the flow of your Holy Spirit and when I experience the happiness that comes from trusting you, help me to express gratitude.

In Jesus' Name,
Amen

## Interaction

Your Prayer:

God's Response:

# 10

# Hope

**Hebrews 6:18-19, 10:23**

# Hope Prayer

Father,

I desire to have an unshakable hope today, that is like a strong, unbreakable anchor holding my soul to you alone. That anchor is tied to your mercy that I find in the secret place. So many great things are hidden in you, and I desire to experience all of them. I desire to know you, to really know you as you are, without any hinderances or distractions. I feel like when I try to get close to you all hell breaks loose in my life, but if I can hold onto this unshakable hope, I will know that I'm not alone, good is coming and I can find rest in you. Wrap my heart tightly around the hope that lives within, as I become settled in the truth that you always keep your promises, and you can never fail. You are a great God and when I walk around with that perspective, I am more confident, because I know the God of the Universe has my back. Your power surrounds me and builds strength in my heart and defeats the enemy every time. Thank you for the peace and renewal that comes when I put my hope in you.

In Jesus' Name,
Amen

# Interaction

Your Prayer:

God's Response:

# 11

# Humility

**James 3:13**

# Humility Prayer

Father,

I realize that humility is so important to you. Jesus gave me the example of true humility when he lowered himself to the position of a servant, a helpless babe, and give up divinity, just to sacrifice himself for humanity. I can't imagine that kind of sacrifice, all because of love. I want love to be what drives me to sacrifice and to not think of myself too highly. Help me not to brag or boast about the things I've done, but instead to always give you the honor and the glory you deserve for all you've done and acknowledge your presence and power in my life. Help me to be willing to sacrifice the things that I want, so that I may live for you. Help me to walk with you in obedience and to seek to please you by how I live my life and always give you the credit you are due. You make all things possible in my life and I don't ever want to take you for granted. Help me to always be aware of your presence and to let your love flow through me to reach others who need to know that you love them too. Make me a willing vessel and a conduit of your love and power, so that others may see you, worship you and give you all the glory.

In Jesus' Name,
Amen

**Interaction:**

Your Prayer:

God's Response:

# 12

# Kindness

Ephesians 4:32

# Kindness Prayer

Father,

I never really thought of it like this, but a way to express kindness to someone is by graciously forgiving them. I always thought of kindness as being nice to someone, even at my own expense, but I don't think that's it at all. Teach me what kindness really is and help me to live with a heart of kindness towards others. I want to live in such a way that being kind is second nature to me as I care for others and seek to bless their heart instead of caring so much about how I can get my own needs met. You say in your word that he who refreshes others will be refreshed and that what I sow I will reap, so help me to sow kindness and generosity even when it is inconvenient. Help me to be gracious in extending forgiveness to others, knowing that I have been graciously forgiven by you. Help me never to withhold affection from my brothers and sisters in Christ, but to give it generously because in doing so I get to experience your presence of love being expressed through me. And when you show up incredible things happen. Kindness is a fruit of your Spirit, so when I express kindness, I get to be a reflection of you, which is what you've made me to be. Help me not to lose sight of this truth and to be mindful of the importance of passing kindness on to others.

In Jesus' Name,
Amen

# Interaction

Your Prayer:

God's Response:

# 13

# Listening

**James 1:19**

# Listening Prayer

Father,

I want to be quick to listen, because it's so easy to miss things which lead to misunderstandings that can easily spiral out of control. I don't want to live in that chaos. Bless me with a desire to listen more than I speak in my interactions with others. Grant me the grace to hear the truth and accept it, instead of walking in denial over the things I am not willing to face. Help me to be quiet as I listen for you, so that yours is the loudest voice in my head and heart. When you speak, I want to embrace your words as the most important so help me to cling to those words as if my life depended on it, because it does. Your words bring life and hope and peace, so if I listen for you and do what you say, I will reap the fruits of that acceptance. Help me to remember that even when you ask a hard thing, it's only to lead me to the good that you are attempting to bring into my life. Even when you ask me to wait, as hard as that is sometimes, it's only ever for my good, because a blessing received too soon becomes a burden too heavy to carry. So, as you're getting me ready for the things you have ready for me, grant me a heart that is eager to listen to you and walk in obedience, no matter the cost.

In Jesus' Name,
Amen

# Interaction

Your Prayer:

God's Response:

# 14

# Mercy

Psalm 103:8-10

Matthew 5:7

# Mercy Prayer

Father,

You are so merciful to me. You've are continually kind to me, tenderhearted and patient with me, who has failed you more times than I can count. When I sin and do the things that break your heart, you still respond with love and care, and you extend mercy when I come to you and admit my sin. You don't treat me the way my sin deserves and for that I am so grateful. I know you cause me to reap the consequences for my behavior so that I will learn and hopefully not make the same mistakes again. But even when I do, you discipline me because you love me and because I'm your child. You want more for me than I can conceive of and in your mercy, you stretch me and help me let go of the things I'm holding onto so tightly in my hands, so that you can give me better things. The limiting life I hold onto, settling only for the crumbs, is not what you want for me. You desire to give me wholeness and a new life and a perspective that says I'm worth more than the crumbs, so I'll hold out for better. Thank you for your mercy. As I have received so much mercy from you, mercies that are new every morning, help me to let your mercy flow like a river out of me to others. Let mercy come and go in my life like a revolving door, so that I continually give and receive it in my life. You give me opportunities to store up mercy, because you know how much I need it. Help me to see those moments of opportunity for what they are and to be quick to extend mercy to the one who is acting out of their brokenness, just as I do.

In Jesus' Name,

Amen

## Interaction

Your Prayer:

God's Response:

# 15

# Obedience

Philippians 2:12

James 2:8

# Obedience Prayer

Father,

You say in your word that if I love you, I will obey you. You also say that obedience is a sacrifice. Well, I want you to know more than anything that I love you and I'm willing to demonstrate that love by doing what you ask me to do, even when it's hard. You've called me to a life that is not easy and sometimes I give into my anger and start to become rebellious. Deep down, it's like I want to hurt you because I'm hurting, but that is not right, and it goes against my desire to show you that I really do love you. Help me in those moments, to seek hard after your presence and receive the power that comes from being exposed to your love. It's when I soak in your love that I can make it through the trials, and it becomes easier to do the things you're leading me to do. Help me to live in a holy awe of you, that draws me into your presence and captivates my heart, so that I walk in obedience consistently. My calling is to obey your command to love you, myself, and my neighbor. As I obey you in this way, would you keep my heart close to you so that nothing and no one can disrupt what I have with you. Help me to be willing to give up what I want, to follow what you want for me because you know me and you know what is best for me and that I'm most fulfilled when I'm walking closely with you, doing what is right. As I cling to your word, may I find the perspective that keeps me walking in obedience to you.

In Jesus' Name,

Amen

## Interaction

Your Prayer:

God's Response:

# 16

# Patience

**Psalm 40:1**

**Romans 8:25**

# Patience Prayer

Father,

Help me to be patient as I wait for you to deliver me. It's your presence that I need, because when you show up, everything changes. I wait patiently for you because I know that you hear me and will answer me. You come through for me in ways that blow my mind and make me want to pinch myself because it feels like a dream. I'm so grateful for the ways you have answered me in the past and I can look back and see a track record of your faithfulness and that gives me hope. As I wait for the fulfillment of your promise to me that fun and laughter and dancing would be my experience in the future, help me to keep worshipping you and keep serving you faithfully. Thank you for the trials that you have used to develop patience in me, so that when it's time to wait I can operate in that mode with ease as I trust you. I realize that for me trusting you is what makes patience possible. Because I trust that you will respond, I can wait patiently and put my focus on the tasks you've given me instead of worrying about something that I cannot control. There are some things only you can do, so I ask that you help me to see when that is the case and to seek you for help instead of striving after something that is beyond me. When you ask me to be patient and trust your timing, help me to be faithful to do that and to praise you in the process.

In Jesus' Name,
Amen

## Interaction

Your Prayer:

God's Response:

# 17

## Peace

Philippians 4:6-7

# Peace Prayer

Father,

I find myself wondering about so many things and it causes me to be distracted when I come to spend time with you. I don't want to be distracted. I want to give you my full attention, because you've been so good to me and because you love me so much and my heart is aware of that. It's you who gives me peace and comfort when I need it. I know that I can come to you with anything and everything and you hear me and respond with mercy and kindness. I am so grateful that I don't have to be worried about anything because I have the freedom to bring everything before you and because you've been faithful to respond in the past, I can trust that you'll continue to be faithful now.

So, I ask that you be with me through every moment of every day. I ask that you teach me how to love you the way you deserve to be loved and show me how to love myself and those around me. I want to walk with you and "offer faith-filled requests before you with overflowing gratitude." Teach me how to receive your peace that allows me to transcend my problems and find you there with me. Let your peace be a protection for my heart and let me rest in the truth of your love and grace today and forever.

In Jesus' Name,
Amen

## Interaction:

Your Prayer:

God's Response:

# 18

## Renewal

### Ephesians 4:22-24

# Renewal Prayer

Father,

You make me brand new by every revelation that's been given to me by you. As I've come to you in prayer and asked you to help me with the things that continually trip me up or keep me bound, you've been faithful to answer me and to remove the clutter from my head. You've revealed your truth to me, that set me free and gave me a new perspective with which to face life. Thank you for the renewal you've given me and for the continual process of transformation that happens in my heart and mind as I seek you and spend time in your presence. Christ is my new life and union with him is what I desire. Thank you that I belong to you in the realm of true holiness and because I belong to you, I get all the benefits of being your child. I have a great inheritance, both here and in eternity and I can receive all the spiritual blessings that make living an empowered life possible. As you make me new, let your incredible power flow through me and transform not just my life, but the lives of everyone connected to me.

In Jesus' Name,

Amen

# Interaction

Your Prayer:

God's Response:

# 19

## Solitude

**Psalm 91:1**

# Solitude Prayer

Father,

When I get alone with you, it's there that I discover how much you know me and love me. When I abide under your shadow, it's there that I am hidden and kept safe and secure. This is where I want to be, out of the reach of the enemy. When I stay close to you, you keep me in the eye of the storm, and you never leave me alone. Sometimes when I'm in the storm, all I see are the winds and the waves and I struggle to fix my eyes on you, the One who calms the storm. I tend to run away, thinking if I go backwards, I can outrun the storm that seems to be chasing me. But it's really the opposite; if I turn my eyes to you and keep walking forward with you, I'll make it to the center, where things are calm and my heart has peace, not because my circumstances have changed, but simply because you're holding my hand and you've told me it's going to be alright. This is what happens when I come to you and seek you in solitude. You meet me there and you strengthen me, and you give me a word to steady me. Thank you for the power that is in the words you speak to me. It changes everything. Help me to hold onto what I receive from you in solitude and treat it as precious, keeping it close to my heart.

In Jesus' Name,
Amen

# Interaction

Your Prayer:

God's Response:

# 20

## Trust

Proverbs 3:5-6

Isaiah 26:3-4

# Trust Prayer

Father,

Fix my thoughts on you and help me to trust you instead of what I can understand with my own mind. I want to trust you completely, because it's there that I find the peace that calms my heart and mind. Lord, there are many things I need to trust you for, but right now I need to trust you with my heart and the things I feel are out of my control. When I experience a longing for things that I can't have right now, would you turn my eyes toward you and change my perspective, so that I see the situation the way you do. Give me faith, to trust what you are doing in my life, to believe that you have a good plan for my life and that when I follow your way my heart will be completely satisfied, lacking no good thing. Guide me in every decision I make and lead me down the path the brings me to abundant life. Thank you for being my rock, my strength, and my peace today. I'm grateful that I can always come to you and put my trust in you, because you never fail me. I trust you because you're undefeated and no one can conquer you. So, in your strength, I find rest for my weary soul that's always trying to figure things out and take charge. But in this I must submit to you and trust that what is for me will be for me and no one can remove from your hand the things you intend to give me. Let my trust in your plan bring you joy and me a continual flow of peace.

In Jesus' Name,
Amen

## Interaction

Your Prayer:

God's Response:

# 2

# Relationships

# 21

## Approval

**1 Thessalonians 2:4**

# Approval Prayer

Father,

Your approval is the only one I want to matter in my life, but I struggle with this. From the time I was little I wanted to please my parents and I thought if I was the perfect daughter, I would always have their approval. That's an exhausting way to live and it left me being a people pleaser. I know that's not the way you want me to live. I believe you want me to live for an audience of One, to seek to live my life in such a way that pleases you and you alone. You made me, you know me, and you want me, just as I am. Would you examine my heart and perform surgery? Remove the lies I've believed and replace them with the truth, that I am wholly and dearly loved by you no matter what and I don't need anyone else's approval but yours to feel like I am enough. I am enough because I am your daughter. I am enough because you made me complete in you. Help me to walk in that reality and trust that you approve of me.

In Jesus' Name,

Amen

## Interaction

Your Prayer:

God's Response:

# 22

# Belonging

## 1 John 2:3-6

# Belonging Prayer

Father,

Help me to settle in my heart that I belong to you. It's the best place to be because in you I find love, in you I find peace, in you I find my purpose and in you I experience a sense of belonging. I know you love me and I fit with you. Because I belong to you, I experience the greatest satisfaction in expressing how much I love you too. The best way I know how to love you is to obey you. Your word says "the love of God will be perfected within the one who obeys God's word" and that is my desire. I want your precious love to be perfected within me, because that's where I find my identity. I am the one who is the beloved daughter of God. Help me never to forget that. I am precious because I am yours and you sing over me. My name is written in the palm of your hand, and no one can pull me away from you. Grant me a perspective that keeps me remaining with you even when the enemy comes after me and tries to convince me that if you cared you wouldn't let bad things happen to me. I recognize that belonging to you means I'm going to experience some trials and sorrow in this life, but it also means you'll always be with me in it. And because Jesus has already overcome the world, the sooner I remember that in my trials, the sooner I can come to a place of celebration and worship even before my circumstances have changed. This is the power I possess because I belong to you. Keep this in the forefront of my mind and help me to find my way to worship, because in it I find you, the one who sustains me. And in this intimate relationship, I understand what it means to be one. Oneness with you is what I desire. It's where I belong. It's where I get to see your heart. Help me never to lose this desire for you.

In Jesus' Name,

Amen

## Interaction

Your Prayer:

God's Response:

.

# 23

# Boundaries

### Micah 6:8

# Boundaries Prayer

Father,

When I think about boundaries, I think about limits that I put on myself that protect me as well as define who I am. I struggle in this area because I want to be loved and accepted and I'm afraid that if I say no to someone it will upset them. So, I say yes at my own expense and then end up getting hurt anyway. Please help me to get out of this unhealthy pattern. Show me how to have healthy boundaries. In your word you set up some healthy boundaries that I want to start living within. You tell me what you require, these are your boundaries for your people and I want to embrace them completely because I believe in doing that I will experience your protection and covering. You call me to do what is right, to love mercy and to walk humbly with you. That is my desire today. I want to do what is right because it pleases you and in doing what is right it will keep me from falling into some unnecessary traps of the enemy. I want to love mercy, not just because I need a lot of it, but because it is your heart to extend mercy to us because you know how flawed we are and how easy it is to go down the wrong path. Teach me to love mercy and to extend it to myself and others instead of judgement. Grant me the desire to walk humbly with you always, not just when you're blessing me or when I feel you close. As I walk closely with you, I know I will experience incredible things that will draw others to you. In the midst of that, keep me humble and never thinking I'm better than anyone else because of the experiences I have with you. You don't play favorites, so what I have with you is available to anyone. Help me to remember that and to keep things in their proper perspective. Bless me with the ability to follow my heart and be who you created me to be no matter what other people think of me. Thank you for the boundaries that exist in your word, boundaries that the enemy cannot cross. As I live within your boundaries, solidify your word in my heart and keep me safe.

In Jesus' Name,
Amen

## Interaction

Your Prayer:

God's Response:

# 24

# Conflict

**Romans 12:18 (NLT)**

# Conflict Prayer

Father,

You desire me to live at peace with everyone and that can sometimes be a hard task. Conflict scares me because I'm so afraid it will turn into abuse. But I know now that you've given me your Spirit to overcome my fears and with that comes wisdom to know how to handle situations where conflict arises. You know the best way to handle tough situations and if I come to you right away, you will grant me the right perspective and give me eyes to see the solution that leads to peace. Grant me the grace to come to you immediately when strife attempts to rear its' ugly head; before I allow harsh or critical words to drive me to distraction. Grant me eyes to see the enemy's attack, so that I don't react in anger or seek to retaliate when someone hurts me. Help me to see the truth behind people's words and actions and respond with love, mercy, and grace, so that I can diffuse a situation. Give me a heart of understanding and compassion in those turbulent moments, to remain calm, to intentionally speak peace and to forgive no matter what.

In Jesus' Name,
Amen

## Interaction

Your Prayer:

God's Response:

# 25

# Confrontation

2 Timothy 2:24-25

# Confrontation Prayer

Father,

I see from your Word that you don't want me to be argumentative, but instead gentle and patient. Often my problem is actually the opposite. I hate confrontation because I fear the abuse that could happen, but I know you don't want me to be afraid of anyone. You are my protection and I believe that if I seek you for wisdom, you will guide me with the right way to address situations that require my attention. Please help me not to back down in fear, but instead to have courage and speak words seasoned with your grace. Grant me the wisdom to know when it's necessary to speak up and when it's better to extend grace and mercy and let a matter go. The truth is important, but so is love. As I seek to help others see the truth, help me to do it with love and care, never forgetting how patient you've been with me. Help me to see confrontation as an opportunity to practice humility with effective communication and a merciful heart.

In Jesus' Name,
Amen

# Interaction

Your Prayer:

God's Response:

# 26

# Envy

James 4:2

# Envy Prayer

Father,

I find myself envious of mothers who get to be with their kids, because that is not the experience I get to have. Granted my daughter is still alive and we are not estranged, but we don't get to live together and that breaks my heart. I had this idea in my head of what motherhood was supposed to look like and when that picture was shattered, it shook my world. Now, when I see mothers interacting with their children, I get jealous and begin to envy what they have. I don't want to be this way because it only steals my joy. For reasons that I don't understand, you have chosen for me to be apart from my daughter and to have a nontraditional relationship with her. It's a sacrifice that leaves me tenderhearted, but I choose to trust you in it and thank you for protecting my daughter and keeping her safe, even from me. Help me not to envy mothers who get to be with their kids, but instead to make the most of every moment I get to be with my daughter and to lean into your comfort when grief and sadness overtake me because of what I have lost. Keep envy and jealousy from poisoning my heart and help me to be grateful for all that you have given me.

In Jesus' Name,
Amen

# Interaction

Your Prayer:

God's Response:

# 27

## Family

Psalm 68:5-6

# Family Prayer

Father,

You called me out from my family at a young age and you've been my constant companion. You've also given me family everywhere you've taken me. You taught me that family does not have to be blood. When I've been lonely, you've provided friends who have become closer to me than family. You've helped me to feel at home with my closest friends and that has been the greatest blessing. I never want to take that for granted. Lord, my heart still longs for a family of my own. While more kids may not be in my future, the desire for a life partner is still there. And while my heart aches for my daughter, for us to live together as a family, I realize that's not what you have for me right now and I need to find my way to accept that. Bring us closer together in such a way that the distance cannot destroy our relationship. Grant us peace and hearts that are determined to find our way back to each other in time.

In Jesus' Name,
Amen

# Interaction

Your Prayer:

God's Response:

# 28

# Forgiveness

## Colossians 3:13

# Forgiveness Prayer

Father,

Forgiveness is so important to you. You left us a very powerful example of forgiveness when Jesus asked you to forgive the ones who were crucifying him, recognizing that they had no idea what they were doing. Jesus had the perspective to see the enemy behind their actions and he was quick to forgive and to intercede for them while they were killing him. What an amazing display of love and an understanding, discerning heart. I remember years ago when you told me that forgiveness is about looking beneath the surface of what was done and seeing the underlying factors. Your words were so important to me at that moment that I can never forget them. You said "take a closer look and don't be so quick to dismiss someone and not forgive them. Walk in forgiveness, because you have no idea what's behind the surface, only I do, and I say forgive." Lord, help me to take these words to heart and always walk in forgiveness, no matter how hurt I feel in the moment. Help me to see the enemy at work behind the scenes, and to put things in their proper perspective. Help me to have a heart that is quick to come to you to work through the issues created by someone else's actions against me and be quick to forgive. Help me to be wise in how I interact with the one I've forgiven and grant me the grace to live with a heart surrendered to you and the way you do things.

In Jesus' Name,
Amen

## Interaction

Your Prayer:

God's Response:

# 29

# Friendship

**Proverbs 18:24**

# Friendship Prayer

Father,

I desire friendships that are closer than family to me. I believe that in true friendship, you can say what needs to be said without fear that the relationship won't survive it. I want to be so secure in the love that exists in those friendships, that I feel safe and can receive that love without hesitation. Bless my friendships and develop in me a desire to be this kind of friend to the people you've brought close to my heart. Help me to steward these friendships well and nurture them with words of encouragement and affirmation. Help me to build up and not tear down. Help me to speak words that breathe life into dying dreams. May I never take my friends for granted. Most importantly I ask that you bless my friendship with you. Help me to be the kind of friend that you can trust with your heart. As I acknowledge your sacrifice, let me feel a kinship with you. May I always appreciate you and never treat you as common or replaceable. There is no one who can take your place in my life. Help me to live from that reality every day and seek to do the things that please your heart and make you feel as special and treasured as you are to me.

In Jesus' Name,

Amen

# Interaction

Your Prayer:

God's Response:

# 30

# Husband

## 1 Corinthians 7:34

# Husband Prayer

Father,

If I'm honest, I have to tell you that I do still want a husband. I know you have been a husband to me all these years and I'm grateful for the ways you have taken care of me, but Lord I miss the things that come with having a husband. I miss the security and not having to carry the responsibilities of life that seem so overwhelming to me at times. I miss the closeness and the intimacy that come with physical touch. I long for that. I know you have provided some of that through others, but it's not the same. I want more than what I have right now, and I know that you can provide it. You made me to know and be known deeply by someone, I have to believe that. I don't want to be alone. Would you meet this desire in my heart and bless me with a good man, who knows you and loves you more than anything else? And when he comes and captures my heart, help me never to lose my first love; YOU who taught me what love was and showed me how to give it away. Thank you that I can tell you the truth and you hear me and don't condemn me. I want to believe that desiring a husband is not rejecting you, but only wanting to experience all that comes with being human. You said it is not good for man to be alone and all I want is to meet that need in the man you have for me. Prepare me Lord for the one you are preparing for me and help me to trust you in the waiting, that it would not be strenuous, but instead filled with a pleasant anticipation of good things to come.

In Jesus' Name,

Amen

## Interaction

Your Prayer:

God's Response:

# 31

## Intimacy

**Genesis 5:24**

# Intimacy Prayer

Father,

I desire intimacy with you more than anything else. Enoch walked with you in close fellowship, so much so that he disappeared from the earth because you took him. That is so attractive to me, to desire you so much that I don't want to walk away from you, no matter what trouble I experience. I want to walk in close fellowship with you, not just because you desire that from me, but because when I'm close to you I feel complete and capable of living this life. When I'm close to you, I feel more like myself, like I can be the best version of myself. I'm afraid of who I would become without you. You make me brave; you give me hope, you inspire me to want to do good things in the world, and in you I feel valuable. There's no one else who can do that for me. God, I have to admit that part of wanting to be that close to you is so that you would take me away from here, from a life of pain and struggle, but I'm beginning to realize that you want to walk with me through it and bring me into beautiful places where pain does not have to continue to be my story. You give beauty for ashes and if I continue to walk with you, I'm certain I will see and get to experience that beauty in my life. In that intimacy with you, I am home. Thank you for showing me how to express my heart to you and for teaching me how to listen when you speak and recognize your voice amidst the chaos. Help me to share every part of my heart with you and not hold anything back.

In Jesus' Name,

Amen

## Interaction

Your Prayer:

God's Response:

# 32

# Love

**1 Corinthians 13:4-7**

# Love Prayer

Father,

When I think about this scripture in 1 Corinthians 13, known as the love chapter, most commonly read at weddings, I think about it from a different perspective. I know that you are love, you are the essence of love itself, so when I read these verses, I see how they tell me about who you are. You are patient, gentle, kind, not selfish or easily irritated or offended. You celebrate honesty and don't find delight in what is wrong. You are a safe place, and you never stop believing the best. You never take failure as defeat, because you never give up. You're never going to stop coming after me, to show me who you are, because you never give up on me. You want me to experience the fullness of who you are and in order to do that I must go through things that present opportunities for you to show up and reveal yourself to meet that need. If I don't need provision, how will you get to show yourself as my provider? I know it may seem like a backwards way to look at it, but if I'm willing to be patient and do without for a season while you are preparing to reveal yourself in the very way I've been needing to see you, then I am sure I will experience relief and blessing. So, help me to be patient while you work behind the scenes to show yourself strong on my behalf. Help me to see your love in all things and receive it that way. Let love be the melody for the song you are singing over my life. Help me to hear it today and every day.

In Jesus' Name,

Amen

## Interaction

Your Prayer:

God's Response:

# 33

# Motherhood

1 Kings 3:26-27

# Motherhood Prayer

Father,

Motherhood is such a touchy subject for me. I feel like I've been stripped of my right to be a mother and that is so painful. While I am so grateful that my daughter is alive and I do still get to interact with her regularly, we don't have the relationship I thought we would. It's painful not to get to live with her and be involved with her daily life. I had so many hopes for what motherhood would be like and that was snatched from me, and it hurts so much that sometimes it's hard to breathe. It's a sacrifice not to get what I want in this part of my life, but I love her, and I want her to live and to have the best life possible. Right now, that is not with me, and my hope and prayer is that in time you would bring us back together and restore the bond we once had and make it even better. In my absence, would you comfort my daughter when moments get hard for her, and she catches a glimpse of what she's missing out on. Bring mother figures into her life who will love her and accept her and teach her the things I'm not getting to. Help me to stand when the pain gets too intense. Give me a word of hope to stand on and let your presence calm the storm in my soul when the grief feels unbearable. Help me to run to you in those moments, tell you how I'm really feeling and sit in the stillness with you until your peace comes. Thank you for meeting me and not leaving me alone to face such a difficult life circumstance. Help me to be grateful that my daughter is alive even if she doesn't get to be with me. I see that for me, motherhood is about sacrifice, so help me to stand strong and continue to believe that this sacrifice I'm making will produce something great in my daughter's life. Draw her to you Lord and may she know the sweetness of your presence and your powerful hand to hold her through every experience she faces.

In Jesus' Name,

Amen

# Interaction

Your Prayer:

God's Response:

# 34

# Needs

Matthew 5:3

Philippians 4:19

2 Peter 1:3

# Needs Prayer

Father,

I recognize how desperately I need you now and always. I am lost without you. You say that happiness and blessing come when I can admit my need for you. Well, I want to walk with you in happiness and blessing, instead of sadness or the curse of a negative mindset. I need your perspective in my life, and I know that as I walk with you, my mind will change and I'll begin to see things with a fresh set of spiritual eyes. With those eyes I can look at my circumstances and bless you for satisfying every need I will ever have. I am so blessed because I have Jesus and the inheritance that will be mine in eternity is so great that I can't even begin to wrap my mind around it. I'm so excited for the glory that will be revealed when I get to see Jesus face to face and walk into the place you have prepared for me in Heaven. But until that time, I will trust you to provide for me and believe that you've deposited in me everything I will need for life and godliness, by your divine power. The more I get to know you, the more I can trust in you and the richer the experiences I will have, which enhance the quality of my life. Thank you for the invitation to come to you and for meeting me right where I'm at and changing my life forever!

In Jesus' Name,
Amen

## Interaction

Your Prayer:

God's Response:

# 35

## Relationships

**Proverbs 17:17**

# Relationships Prayer

Father,

Relationships can be so tricky. There are times when I desire relationships and there are times when I just want to be alone. I struggle with balance in this area of my life because for so long I isolated myself from other people, but now as you've been healing me and helping me to overcome my fears, I realize I desire connection and I'm willing to take the risk to have it in my life. As I seek out healthy relationships with others, please guide me, protect me and grant me discernment, so that I let the good in and keep the bad out. Bless my family relationships as well and help me to continue to develop in and through them. You've given me family, by blood and you've given me family in the body of Christ and I'm grateful for both. Please have your way in the relationships I have with my brothers and sisters in Christ, that love would be evident. Help us to support each other and pray for each other regularly and carry each other's burdens, so that life becomes more manageable. You give us each other for a reason. When the enemy comes to set up traps, it's those relationships that provide insight and your power shows up as we pray together and put the devil to shame. Grant me the grace to walk into these relationships with love and respect and to treat them as sacred, but also to remember that my most important relationship is the one I have with you. It's because of this relationship that I can even function in this life. I'm open to others because of what you've done in my heart. Continue to transform me and guide me as I grow in my relationships and care for those you've put in my path.

In Jesus' Name,

Amen

## Interaction

Your Prayer:

God's Response:

# 36

## Selfishness

**James 3:15-16**

# Selfishness Prayer

Father,

I struggle so much with selfishness. The things I've experienced in my life have caused me to be so focused on myself, on my hurt and pain over the things done to me. I've become so accustomed to thinking about myself that I forget you have the power to free me from that bondage. Selfishness is a prison that keeps me bound when I'm not willing to consider others and what they need. It's not all about me and the world does not revolve around me, even when I like to think it does. Set me free from selfishness today and help me to see that you take care of me and you provide the things I need, so I don't have to obsess over my life. Self-awareness is important when it leads me to you, but too much focus on myself only leads to self-absorption and jealousy. When I'm jealous, I want what someone else has and I live from a place of entitlement that is not pleasing to you. Please help me to be completely content with where you have me and with what you've given me. And when I have a need or desire, help me to speak up and ask you for it instead of complaining about what I don't have or what I don't like in my life. Grant me the grace to walk with a satisfied heart and an open hand to give to others, so that selfishness does not rule my life.

In Jesus' Name,
Amen

# Interaction

Your Prayer:

God's Response:

# 37

# Vulnerability

## Matthew 26:37-39

# Vulnerability Prayer

Father,

I believe that when I'm vulnerable with you, you will come to meet me and angels will appear to strengthen me. It's not easy to be vulnerable because it means admitting things to myself that I'm not always ready to accept. But you give me the ability and the desire to turn to you when I'm overwhelmed and tell you how I'm really feeling. There's nothing too hard for you to hear from me and I'm grateful that I can express myself to you without condemnation. In the moments where I express my heart to you, please protect me from the thoughts that would cause me to shrink back in fear. Help me to trust that you will meet me right where I'm at and minister to me. And when the time comes for me to be vulnerable with others, grant me wisdom and discernment to know who I can share my heart with and who I cannot. Not everyone has earned the right to know the details, but you've given me some who can be trusted. Give me the courage to share and a heart that will be healed from the interaction.

In Jesus' Name,

Amen

# Interaction

Your Prayer:

God's Response:

# 3

# Challenges to Overcome

# 38

# Abandonment

**Psalm 9:10**

# Abandonment Prayer

Father,

You know I am no stranger to abandonment. It has been a deep experience in my life and it's communicated to me that I must not be worth loving, that I'm not important enough to stick it out with. The message I've received is that I don't deserve love in this life. But, I'm beginning to see that no matter what rejection I've experienced in my life, you have never abandoned me. You came close in my pain, and you made sure I didn't go through the aftermath of that heart-break alone. You loved me in my brokenness, and you stuck it out when I began to question your love for me and went after other things to fill the holes inside. You were patient with me when I struggled to love you. You were kind to me when I didn't know how to be kind to myself. You showed up as King in my life and you took the pain of abandonment and feeling discarded as worthless away from me. You treated me as precious and valuable. You gave me my worth back and for that I will always be grateful. I commit myself to you because you showed me who I really am, a masterpiece, a beautiful vessel set aside for special use. You made me worthy of love and I can bring all my tears to you and you treat every one as precious to you. I not only have tears of pain, but because of your love I cry tears of joy and gratitude. Thank you for saving me. Thank you for loving me. Thank you for coming close and forgiving me for the times that I hurt your heart. Your mercy covers me, so I choose to put my trust in you and kneel in the safety of your presence.

In Jesus' Name,

Amen

# Interaction

Your Prayer:

God's Response:

# 39

# Change

**Romans 12:2**

# Change Prayer

Father,

I want you to change me from the inside out. I realize that requires me to submit to your process of changing the way I think and how I approach life, not just in the challenges, but even in experiencing the good things. I don't want to look like the world. I want to stand out and be a light for you that draws people into your love and mercy. In order to do that, I need your perspective. Help me to see you working in my life and to accept that sometimes rejection is protection, because you see what I do not, and you protect my heart from the things I'm not ready to experience yet. Transform me by the power of your Holy Spirit so that I operate in this life with precision and grace, to stand on your word and use it to tear down the thoughts in my head that are not from you. Break the thought patterns that keep me from walking in the destiny you created for me before the foundations of the world. Thank you that you knew me before I came here and you're sustaining me and developing me as I walk with you. In this transformation, may I know and experience your miraculous power that is so explosive it changes the world. Teach me to pray and live in such a way that it sparks not just a change in me, but a change in the world where those who have been looking for something to fill the emptiness inside will find you, and in that a satisfaction that is contagious.

Bring this kind of change that spreads like wildfire throughout the earth!

In Jesus' Name,
Amen

## Interaction

Your Prayer:

God's Response:

# 40

## Crisis

Psalm 28:7

# Crisis Prayer

Father,

Thank you for being my strength and my shield. In moments of crisis, you've been there to steady me. I've seen you come through time and time again when I've cried out to you for help. You were quick to come to my aid, not allowing me to think for one moment that you didn't care. Your presence has been one of the greatest gifts of my life. When you're with me I feel like I can climb the highest mountain and overcome the darkness that tries to overshadow my life. When I'm falling apart, I feel your embrace through the warmth of a friend and I'm encouraged and energized to keep moving forward. Knowing who you've been to me, my heart can't help but praise you and express how much I love you. I can have joy as I worship you, even when my circumstances would say differently. You shield me from the impact of collateral damage that exists in the battle between good and evil. I trust you to uphold me, so I'll sing praises to bless your heart. I ask Lord that you would grant me eyes that are quick to look to heaven when crisis comes knocking on my door, and a heart that does not faint, but instead calls out to you with determination and faith.

In Jesus' Name,
Amen

# Interaction

Your Prayer:

God's Response:

# 41

# Depression

**Proverbs 13:12**

# Depression Prayer

Father,

Sometimes it gets so dark that I can't find my way to your light. I lose all hope and with that my will to keep on living. Somehow the enemy convinces me that it would be better if I wasn't around and that I'm a burden to the all the people close to me. I get so discouraged and when the enemy attacks I feel like I can't take one more thing. I lose all confidence in my ability to handle life. It's gets too overwhelming for me and I just want to escape it all. But somehow, you cut through all the noise in my head and speak ever so softly that you are here and you love me. You speak words of life and give me a sense of purpose that lets me know you're not done with me yet; there's still work for me to do here and a sweetness of life for me to experience. When you told me not to deprive you of the opportunity to wow me, that really got my attention. You have incredible things for me to experience here in this life and if I give up, I will miss out on the abundant life Jesus paid such a dear price for me to experience here on earth. So, Lord I'm asking that you would help me with the depression when it comes to drag me into hell and would you plant a seed of hope in my heart? Give me a word that breaks the back of the enemy's attack on my mind and grant me the grace to stand on that word and be delivered. Thank you for meeting me in those dark places and for not condemning me when I struggle. I bless you for the way you love me through it and hold me when the tears come. You are my savior, my King, my life. Be my strength when I feel weak and break the power of depression over my life.

In Jesus' Name,

Amen

# Interaction

Your Prayer:

God's Response:

# 42

# Distractions

**Hebrews 12:1**

# Distractions Prayer

Father,

You know I am easily distracted. Sometimes I seek out distractions to keep me from dealing with the issues in my heart. I do this because I'm afraid that the pain will be too great or that I'll fall into a pit of depression and never be able to get out of it. I get distracted by sin because I get tired of the fight and my heart tends to wander in those moments. Surely, that is when the enemy presents attractive options, using my loneliness against me. I used to turn to alcohol to distract me, but now that I'm sober that is no longer an option. You desire me to let go of every wound that has pierced me and the sin that I so easily fall into, and I realize these two are connected. If I let go of the wounds, I will be less likely to fall into sin so easily, because those traps will no longer look attractive to me. When I act out of my wounds, I fall into sin, which is why you want me to deal with the wounds in my soul. Only you can help me to do that, so I ask that you help me to let go of the distractions I use as my means of avoidance and to face every wound with courage, addressing the impact of experiences that hurt me deeply and admitting to myself what I've been through. As I acknowledge the reality of the things that happened, would you bring healing and breakthrough, so I can let go of the things I've been holding onto so tightly trying to protect myself from more painful experiences. Show me that I am enough, that pain no longer has to define who I am, and that you can give me a brand-new identity in you, so I can finish the race strong and inspire others to find freedom from their distractions.

In Jesus' Name,

Amen

# Interaction

Your Prayer:

God's Response:

# 43

# Emotions

Proverbs 4:23

Galatians 5:22-23

# Emotions Prayer

Father,

You tell me to guard my heart because it affects all that I am. My heart was damaged before I ever learned how to guard it, so now I experience chaos in my emotions and continual instability. I need you to reverse the effects of that damage so that I can live in balance in my emotions. You give me your Spirit to produce emotions in me that are life-giving, like love, joy, and peace. Sometimes I feel like these things are undermined by my insecurities, so I'm asking that you cause me to be secure in you. If I can be secure in you, I will embrace who you say I am and I won't question myself and other people so much. I realize that the root of my insecurity is uncertainty because of the things I experienced early on in my life. I began to be uncertain that you would keep me safe, that I could survive in the world. Everything was so shaky, my foundation had so many cracks and I couldn't get my footing. I became so unsettled, and worry became the tool I used to protect myself. But this is not your way. You want me to trust in you, to trust that you have my back and you're not going to leave me to fend for myself. I know that when I trust you, my emotions calm down and I experience your peace, but because of my insecurities it doesn't last like you mean for it to. Would you help me Lord? I become afraid that I'm going to get hurt by the enemy, and I back away from you instead of running to you. I don't want to do that anymore. I want to hold onto you. I want my first instinct to be to reach out for you, because if I do that, I know I will find you and my heart will calm down and positive emotions will follow. Grant me the grace to walk in this way.

In Jesus' Name,

Amen

# Interaction

Your Prayer:

God's Response:

# 44

# Failure

**Micah 7:8**

# Failure Prayer

Father,

I feel like I have failed in the greatest way imaginable. I made a choice that had drastic consequences and now I'm living with my failure and it's hard. The loss I feel is great. Lord, help me to rise again after falling. Be my light and pull me out of the darkness. Help me to reflect on my actions in such a way that brings clarity and grant me the ability to be merciful toward myself, to see my failure as an opportunity to learn from my mistakes. In my reflection, keep me from getting down on myself and lead me to your truth. I need your perspective. Help me to understand how I could have made such a big mistake. Help me to deal with the issues in my heart and grant me grace when I act out of my brokenness. Show me how to address the pain in my heart and to bring those feelings to you and to admit the impact that those experiences have had on me. As I bring these things to you, would you circumcise my heart and remove the lies I have believed about myself, other people, the world, and you and give me a clearer picture of reality as you would have me to see it. Let my failure be the catalyst for change, not only in me but in those you have placed in my life to inspire. Reignite the fire within me and let me be the spark that sets someone else's heart ablaze for you.

In Jesus' Name,
Amen

## Interaction

Your Prayer:

God's Response:

# 45

# Fear

## 2 Timothy 1:7

# Fear Prayer

Father,

I've been afraid of so many things most of my life. Fear has been my constant companion and I'm finally getting to the point where I don't want to live like that. I want to be free from living in fear of the unknown, fear of people and the potential for abuse, fear of rejection, fear of abandonment, fear of heartbreak; all the things that keep me from living my life to the fullest. I see how fear has paralyzed me and kept me from taking risks that could lead to beautiful experiences. I thought fear would keep me safe, but really, it's just created a prison that I've lived in my whole life. I know you haven't given me a spirit of fear, it's something the enemy has kept me bound in; but I'm ready to let go of that fear and walk in the power, love and self-control that your Spirit gives to me. Help me to rest in your perfect love that causes fear to leave. I know if I trust in your love for me, I will believe that you surround me with protection, provision, and every good thing and if that's the case, what do I have to be afraid of? You have hosts of angels to keep watch over me. You are not limited in your resources, so in you I have everything that I need to live. And I know that you are good and desire to bless me with good things. I trust that and because I trust that my heart can rest, and I can let go of trying to cover myself and figure everything out. Thank you for this freedom today.

In Jesus' Name,
Amen

## Interaction

Your Prayer:

God's Response:

# 46

# Frustration

Psalm 78: 40-42

# Frustration Prayer

Father,

You have been so good to me. Again and again, you have delivered me, yet still when the trials come I forget what you've done for me and I start to feel like I'm alone and have to figure out a solution by myself. This must create so much frustration for you. I'm sorry. I don't want to do this to you. You don't deserve that. I want my first reaction to be, "lord, help me!" I want to see the trial as an opportunity to show you how much I trust you to be my vindicator. I'm beginning to realize that these trials also give me an opportunity to discover you in a new way. Recently, you revealed yourself to me as King and that was so powerful. Now that I see you as King in my life, I want to trust that in your power nothing is too challenging for you. You can cover me, especially when I make messes that seem to jeopardize my future. This is not too difficult for you and your love for me is too great for you to leave me stranded. I believe that and I will trust that and trust you to take care of me. Grant me your peace as I hold tightly to you in this storm.

In Jesus' Name,

Amen

# Interaction

Your Prayer:

God's Response:

# 47

# Grief

Isaiah 53:3, 10

Ecclesiastes 3:4

# Grief Prayer

Father,

In your expression of love for me, you took all the clutter out of my head; all those experiences of grief, loss and sadness that I collected. You took my pain away as you helped me identify with the One who is completely acquainted with grief. The prayer you told me to pray as I worked through my grief, with a grief counselor, was so powerful to me. "Man of sorrows take my pain and give me peace, beauty for my ashes and double for my trouble." I didn't even realize that prayer came from your word when you gave it to me. But I have seen the fruit of that prayer and in it I experienced a rebirth. Thank you for making me new and for helping me to work through grief when it comes in waves. Grieving is necessary and healthy when loss has occurred and I'm grateful to know that grief has an end, and that dancing will follow. How I long to dance, to be free to embrace joy and laughter. Thank you for your promise to me that it is coming. I look forward to the experience with you. Thank you for your perfect plan.

In Jesus' Name,

Amen

# Interaction

Your Prayer:

God's Response:

# 48

# Loneliness

**Luke 5:16**

# Loneliness Prayer

Father,

I've read that loneliness is a silent killer, but I'm starting to get a picture of how you see loneliness and the way it's designed to function in my life. When I experience loneliness, it's a signal that you are calling to me to satisfy a deficiency that exists in my heart. Only you can fix what's been broken. I've been lonely most of my life, because I isolated myself in an effort to protect me from harm, and that isolation led to chronic depression. It's been a devastating place to be. I know that's not the life you want for me. Jesus often went to the wilderness to pray; that's a lonely place, but there He got to meet you and be satisfied by you. In my loneliness, I haven't spent much time searching for you; instead, I've settled into self-pity and nursed a victim mentality. I've blamed others for my loneliness, instead of realizing that I put myself there. I don't want to do that anymore. I don't want to retreat into myself in that way. I want to reach out and receive the love that you've provided, that is waiting for me in healthy relationships. That requires taking risks, which I'm not always good at, but I ask that you help me in this area to see past my fear, embrace your love and with that the courage to trust the people you've brought to me. Loneliness is my cue to first reach out for you, receive what I need from you and then be open, yet discerning, in my quest for connection. I ask that you heal the damage done by my own isolating behavior and restore me to healthy connections that are full of your love and light.

In Jesus' Name,
Amen

# Interaction

Your Prayer:

God's Response:

# 49

# Loss

Psalm 34:18

Lamentations 3:32

# Loss Prayer

Father,

You know the losses I've experienced, some great and very devastating. Some of these losses I didn't think I would survive, but I'm still here by your grace and because you've been faithful to come close to me in those times. I believe in the restoration of joy that comes as I bring my pain to you. You've shown me that where loss has occurred there is the opportunity for new life to spring forth and that's what I desire to experience. The sadness that comes with loss lets me know that I'm missing something of value, something that mattered to me. I'm grateful to have had something so important in my life, but now what do I do? How do I live without the things and people that have meant so much to me? Only you know. Grant me the grace to walk through loss and find myself on the other side of my grief, where joy and laughter and dancing are restored. Show me your compassion, because of the greatness of your unfailing love.

In Jesus' Name,

Amen

# Interaction

Your Prayer:

God's Response:

# 50

## Mistakes

Genesis 3:12-13

# Mistakes Prayer

Father,

You know I have a tendency to make big mistakes and I think I do that because of my impatience and because I fall prey to deception. There's a belief I have that it's not going to get any better than this, so I might as well take what I can get. That belief drives my impatience, and I become unwilling to wait for the better that you are preparing for me. I become deceived into thinking that you don't see me down here struggling with loneliness or that you are indifferent and don't care. I become driven by lust of the flesh, lust of the eyes and the pride of life and I act out of that place, instead of trusting you to give me the Kingdom. I can see why patience is one of the most important virtues, because it keeps me out of trouble. If I'm willing to wait and willing to trust in your goodness, I will hold out for the better that comes with a life surrendered to you. Keep me from falling into the trap of deception that waits for me. Help me to trust your character.

In Jesus' Name,

Amen

## Interaction

Your Prayer:

God's Response:

# 51

# Pain

Hebrews 2:18

Psalm 126:5-6

# Pain Prayer

Father,

Thank you for the revelation that when I bring you my pain, instead of denying it or trying to drown it out in unhealthy ways, I get to exchange that pain for your power in my life. You give me the ability to overcome as I talk to you about what hurts in my life. Jesus suffered and endured every test and temptation, so that he can help me every time I face the trials of life, but he can't help me if I'm not willing to face it. I must be willing to face the pain instead of run from it and trust that I will not only survive it, but I can give it to you and receive your peace, your perspective and your power. When I receive your peace, my heart calms down and I am open to receive your spiritual sight. When I see things the way you do, I can operate with your faith and your supernatural power will flow through me to touch others and bring great healing. Your power not only brings healing, but it effects the atmosphere. The wind and the waves submit to your power by just a word, so when I allow your faith to operate in my life, I can speak words that move mountains and effect change in the world around me. When I walk in your power, the pain subsides and joy, gladness and blessing become my reward. So I ask that you would help me when I experience pain, to come to you, trust you with my heart and my feelings and receive the word that sets me free from pain's hold on me. It's your power that does what seems impossible and heals my broken heart. Let your peace rest in my heart, grant me your perspective and let your power flow through me right now. Thank you for your peace, your perspective, and your power today!

In Jesus' Name,

Amen

# Interaction

Your Prayer:

God's Response:

# 52

# Past

**Philippians 3:13**

# Past Prayer

Father,

As I think about my past, I am full of regret. I regret the mistakes I've made that have brought so much pain into my life. I regret not taking better care of myself, because that's what led to me getting sick and being unable to care for my daughter. My mistakes and this illness have cost me so much, but it's time to do what your word says and forget all of the past and focus on the future instead. If I keep focusing on the past, I'll waste the opportunity to create a better future by making good choices in my present. Yes, I've made mistakes. Yes, I've been sick, you are a God who is powerful and not limited by my weakness. Lord, you have the power to set me free from my past and to give me a future and a hope that is full of life, joy, and peace. Help me not to live in regret, but instead to learn from my mistakes and to be willing to share what you've taught me with humility and gentleness. I ask now that you would break the chains of my past off my soul and transform my mind so that I focus on the bright future you have created for me. Thank you for setting me free from my past. As I walk in this freedom, when those moments come where the enemy attempts to remind me of my past, may I remind him of his future and keep moving forward in freedom.

In Jesus' Name,
Amen

## Interaction

Your Prayer:

God's Response:

# 53

# Pride

Provers **16:18**

Proverbs **13:10**

# Pride Prayer

Father,

Pride is so dangerous. It scares me. Your word says the higher I lift myself up in pride, the harder I'll fall in disgrace. Well, I don't want to fall in disgrace. I want to keep a level head and a healthy view of myself. Sometimes I struggle to see your perspective when I'm going through difficult things, and I realize that I become prideful and begin to question you and what you're doing in my life. I let my pride get in the way of what you're doing when I'm not willing to be open about my life because I fear being judged. You've done so much for me and your power in my life is evident in my story. Help me not to give into pride and be close-lipped about what you've done for me. You've been my constant companion, how could I deny you what you want, which is to share my testimony with the people you bring to me? Help me also to be open to receive advice from trustworthy people who know you and not be afraid that someone will pick apart my life and tell me everything I'm doing wrong. The root of pride for me is thinking I know better than you, but I obviously don't. Please kill that attitude in me when it begins to surface and keep me humble and dependent on you.

In Jesus' Name,

Amen

# Interaction

Your Prayer:

God's Response:

# 54

# Shame

1 John 1:9

Psalm 34:5

Psalm 119:80

Isaiah 49:23

# Shame Prayer

Father,

I feel shame when I make big mistakes and I know I've disappointed you. I haven't trusted you and I've been impatient and that's led to sin in my life. Please forgive me for my sin and my struggles. I am grateful that you are merciful and gracious to me when I come to you and admit my sin. Your word says that you forgive me because of Christ and you cleanse my heart from all unrighteousness. That is what I need today. I need your grace to give me what I don't deserve. I want to join my life with yours, because that's when joy comes, and I never have to wear the face of shame again. "Make me passionate and wholehearted to fulfill your every wish, so that I'll never have to be ashamed of myself." Another aspect of shame that I am aware of, is when I trust in you, I will never be put to shame. Help me to hold onto that truth and to be quick to trust you and depend on you, even when it looks foolish. Thank you for making it possible for me to never be put to shame again, as I follow your way and seek to live my life in obedience to you. Lord, you are so good and so faithful, how could I not follow you? Thank you for freeing me from the bondage of a shame-filled identity. May I never be caught in that trap again and when I sin, cause me to be quick to confess it to you and receive your forgiveness.

In Jesus' Name,
Amen

## Interaction

Your Prayer:

God's Response:

# 55

## Stress

Psalm 86:7

2 Corinthians 4:9

# Stress Prayer

Father,

Help me to deal with stress in a positive way. When trouble comes, help me to cry out to you because I know you will answer me and come running to help me. You are quick to come to my aid when I put my trust in you. And even when it seems like the walls are closing in on me and there is no way to escape, help me to stop in that moment and ask for you to be present with me. I know that when you come, you come with power and authority and nothing and no one can defeat you. When you enter the flames with me, you release me from every bondage and when you bring me out, I won't even smell like smoke. That lets me know that no matter how long I've been bound by something, when you set me free, I won't even look like what I've been through. So, I can be grateful for stress, because it draws me to you and when I find you the stress releases its hold on me. I know that a certain amount of stress is healthy and necessary for my development, so would you change the way I look at stress so that I'm no longer overwhelmed by it, but instead intrigued by it and what you're going to use it to do in my life. Help me to see stress as an opportunity for me to see you in a different light, to get to know you in a new way and to become someone who gets to witness the demonstration of your power.

In Jesus' Name,
Amen

## Interaction

Your Prayer:

God's Response:

# 56

## Suffering

**1 Peter 5:10**

# Suffering Prayer

Father,

I thank you that suffering is temporary. You promise to be with me in my suffering and I desperately need to believe that is true. Sometimes I get to a place in my suffering where I feel like you are far from me and I get angry with you that life has to be so hard. I don't want to be that way. In my heart I know that you will never leave me and when it feels like you are far away, I realize it's because I have started to walk away from you in my despair, but that's when I need to come closer to you. When I'm in the storm, all I see are the raging waves and the darkness and I feel alone, but I see now that if I lift my eyes to heaven, I can see you watching over me and hear you encouraging me to come back to the path, to come into your presence and feel your strength and your love. I choose to believe your word that you will personally and powerfully restore me and make me stronger than ever. Change my perspective about suffering, so that I cling to you in the midst of my pain and brokenness instead of running from you. In my suffering, give me eyes to see you and ears to hear you and a heart to worship you.

In Jesus' Name,
Amen

## Interaction

Your Prayer:

God's Response:

# 57

## Temptation

### James 1:13-15

# Temptation Prayer

Father,

Temptation takes many forms in my life. Sometimes I'm tempted to give into my desires and not follow your way. Other times I'm tempted to doubt that you care for me or what I'm going through. I'm tempted to give into fear in my relationships, instead of trusting you to protect me and guide me into healthy spaces. When I'm tempted, your word tells me that you are not the author of that temptation. It's my own desires and thoughts that lead me into evil and darkness. I don't want my evil desires to give birth to evil actions, so I ask that you break the cycle of temptation the enemy uses to try to trap me before rebellion fully develops in me. Keep me from following the path to temptation, to see the crossroads when I'm there and to choose life and faith, instead of evil and rebellion. And if the root of temptation is desire, I ask that you uproot the evil desires that lead to destruction and plant good desires in my heart, so that I follow after your way and trust in your good purposes for my life.

In Jesus' Name,

Amen

## Interaction

Your Prayer:

God's Response:

# 4

# Practices

# 58

## Acceptance

Romans 15:7

# Acceptance Prayer

Father,

Thank you for fully accepting me and receiving me as your partner. I want to live a life worthy of that acceptance. I never want you to feel like I wasn't a worthwhile investment. The way you've taken the time to pour into me, to walk with me and to heal me, is incredible to me. I never want to waste the work that you've done in my life by treating you as if you are insignificant. You are the most important part of my life and I want to live my life in such a way that shows I completely accept you. I know that sometimes I experience a temptation to reject you when life gets hard, and I feel like it's your fault that it's hard. But you didn't call me to an easy life. You called me to a life of love that includes sacrifice. It's a sacrifice to obey you sometimes, because I'm choosing your way over my own. It's a sacrifice to love you, because to love you is to open myself up to the attack of the enemy. He wouldn't come after me if I wasn't in relationship with you, reflecting your love and grace in the earth. Lord, I want you to know that I accept you despite the enemy. You are the lover of my soul and the great love of my life. Because I am accepted by you, I am complete and in that understanding, I can accept others. I don't have to reject them because of my fear that they will reject me. Since I know that I am accepted by you, even if they reject me, I can trust that you will provide people in my life who will accept me and welcome me into their lives. Help me to be driven by love and to learn how to accept the good without accepting what is unhealthy. Protect me from getting into relationships that are characterized by control and abuse, thinking I don't deserve better. Show me the kind of relationships you want me to have and help me not to be afraid of intimacy.

In Jesus' Name,
Amen

# Interaction

Your Prayer:

God's Response:

# 59

# Comfort

**2 Corinthians 1:4**

# Comfort Prayer

Father,

There have been so many things that I've experienced in the past that have broken my heart. It's been so hard to endure these things, but what has helped is trusting you to comfort my heart. I know there have been times where I've run from you instead of turning to you in my pain and I realize now that that breaks your heart. You want me to come to you with any pain, because you are the perfect one to comfort me. You are no stranger to pain and heartache because you made the ultimate sacrifice for humanity, to give up your son so we could be saved. I understand that that sacrifice was painful, and you endured it for me. Thank you.

You made me and you know me intimately. You know every fracturing in my heart and mind. Your comfort is the fire that fuses the broken pieces of my heart and mind back together. In your comfort I find peace. In your comfort the pain melts away and I am finally free. Thank you for your comfort. Help me not to forget to pass it on. The comfort you give me builds up a reserve in me that I use to comfort others. Help me not to lose sight of what it means to pay it forward. I've received comfort, I must give it. I've received love, I must let it flow out of me like a river that brings life. Thank you for helping me to see that today. Help me to be that channel of your love, mercy, grace, and comfort that is possible when

I'm connected to you. Help me to stay connected to you, my source for every good thing.

In Jesus' Name,

Amen

## Interaction

Your Prayer:

God's Response:

# 60

## Confession

James 5:16

# Confession Prayer

Father,

Confession is so important to you. I think of David, who came to you from the brokenness in his heart over what he did and acknowledged his sin. I want to be able to come to you in this way when I sin. You know I have a tendency to make big mistakes that hurt your heart and I'm sorry for that. I'm grateful for your mercy when I come to you and admit my wrongdoing. You know I act out of my brokenness and that's not an excuse, it's just the reality of it; but I'm grateful that you make provision for me when I mess up and while I still have to live with the consequences of my actions, you are gracious even then and that blesses my heart. Thank you for giving me friends that I can confess to, and pray with, so that I may experience your healing. Continue to provide those kinds of safe friends for me, so that I never hesitate to speak up and confess when I sin. Keep my heart tender in this area so that I'm not quick to sin or do things that grieve your heart, especially in the trial when I have a tendency to get upset and become rebellious. Let my commitment to you be strong enough to hold me steady when the enemy's attack causes me to question your loving presence in my life. Grant me a resolve to hold onto the truth of your love for me and your good plans for my life especially when I mess up and the enemy tries to tell me you're done with me, that I've messed up too big this time and you can never use me again. Help me to feel your reassurance in those moments and be filled with your peace because of your goodness.

In Jesus' Name,

Amen

## Interaction

Your Prayer:

God's Response:

# 61

# Decisions

**Psalm 25:4**

# Decisions Prayer

Father,

When I have an important decision to make, help me to turn to you and seek you for guidance, wisdom and the ability to make choices with a level head. Direct my steps and teach me how to choose the things that matter most to eternity, instead of investing my time in things that have no lasting value. Help me to strive for things that build your kingdom and not my own. Grant me an understanding heart, that I may see what's important in the moment and have the courage to choose it even if it's unpopular. Help me not to make decisions based on what other people think about me, but instead to choose the right path where I get to walk side by side with you. Help me to make healthy decisions that cause blessings to flow from one generation to the next. Grant me the ability to be intentional about how I express my faith in you to others and to let my actions speak so much louder than any word spoken. I want to live a life that pleases you and is a reflection of your Son on the earth, because the greatest decision I ever made was to believe in the name of Jesus and accept the sacrifice he made to pay for my sin. Thank you for giving me the freedom to make that decision and to discover your love.

In Jesus' name,
Amen

## Interaction

Your Prayer:

God's Response:

# 62

## Energy

Philippians 4:13

# Energy Prayer

Father,

Sometimes I struggle with having enough energy to make it through the day and I need your strength to sustain me. I recognize that part of having enough energy is not wasting it by focusing on things that I cannot control and ruminating or worrying about them all day long. I don't want to live that way and I don't believe you want me to either. I want to make the most of the energy that you give me each day and I know that if I feed my spirit as well as my body with good things, I will have all the energy I need to sustain me, so that I can accomplish the things you've created me to do. Help me to feed on good things for my heart and not waste my energy on thoughts that lead to darkness and depression. Help me to believe in the promises that you have made to me, that you will always be with me and that you've given me your Spirit to strengthen me so that I can overcome every difficulty and still have energy to spare. Let your vitality flow through me and give me power to live completely for you.

In Jesus' Name,

Amen

## Interaction:

Your Prayer:

God's Response:

# 63

## Gratitude

**Psalm 50:23**

# Gratitude Prayer

Father,

Your word says that the life that pleases you is a life lived in the gratitude of grace and when I think about that it makes a lot of sense to me. If I choose to be grateful for the grace that you give me every day, I will see you operating more and more in my life. The more grateful I am, the more I will see and the more my attitude will change to one of hope. So, when depression comes, I choose to express my gratitude for everything I can think of, and I'll watch things begin to change. Gratitude loosens the grip that depression has on my soul. So, I thank you for the power that exists in the words I speak of gratefulness to you. Help me to remember to use this tool early and often when I'm facing an attack from the enemy.

In Jesus' Name,
Amen

# Interaction

Your Prayer:

God's Response:

# 64

## Healing

Malachi 4:2

Isaiah 53:5

# Healing Prayer

Father,

Healing comes from you! I am so grateful for the ways you have healed me and brought a deeper sense of wholeness into my life. I know that I can come to you because you are always available, and you never cease to bring what you know I need. It's in you that I find the healing that sets me free. You call me to come to you, not because you want to control me, but because you want to release me from the shackles that I carry around. You see them more clearly than anyone and you're so gentle in how you remove them. I know that to receive this kind of healing, I have to come close enough for you to touch me and that's scary to me. The pain beneath the shackles is great and I'm afraid if you touch it, it will hurt more. I need courage and your faith to come close enough to you to be set free. Show me that it's not another trap, that I can trust you, that I'm safe with you and if I sit with you for a while I'll begin to heal and get stronger. Then I'll see myself the way you see me as beautiful, elegant and pure and no matter what I've endured no one can take the reality of that identity away from me. Thank you for the healing that comes as I embrace this identity.

In Jesus' Name,
Amen

## Interaction

Your Prayer:

God's Response:

# 65

# Meditation

**Psalm 62:1,5**

# Meditation Prayer

Father,

I see meditation as being still with you, pondering your word and listening to what you want to say to me specifically. In the stillness, all other things fall away and I can sense your presence and hear your voice so clearly. As I meditate on your words, it changes me. There's something so meaningful and powerful in your word that transforms my heart and mind. I desire this transformation because in it I become more aware of who you are, my Savior and King. You make me more like you as I chew on your word and let it marinate in my soul. The more I become like you, the more your power becomes manifest in my life and it touches those who encounter me. I want more of this, because I want to see your Kingdom operating on earth and setting hearts and minds free. Let your healing flow in me to touch others as I get in your presence. May I come to you every day to receive a fresh infilling of your mercy, grace and love and to receive a word from you to guide my day. It's all about you and what you want to do in me and through me. Help me to always remember that and to keep seeking you and meditating on you and your word for it's there that I find my security.

In Jesus' Name,
Amen

## Interaction

Your Prayer:

God's Response:

# 66

# Money

**Hebrews 13:5**

# Money Prayer

Father,

Money has been a scarce resource for a lot of my life and it seems like as soon as money is not an issue something happens to pull me backwards into scarcity. I ask that you remove the scarcity mindset from me and replace it with a kingdom mentality, where I believe your resources are fully at my disposal, and I lack no good thing. Help me to live content with what you have provided for me and to be faithful to be a good steward over my finances. Help me to make good financial decisions and to be generous as you provide for me, to build your kingdom and make a positive impact in the world. Thank you for always having your presence and when I have you, I have everything I could ever need. Thank you for promising to never leave me and for not loosening the grip you have on my life. Because I'm in your hands, I know that I'm safe and you won't allow me to fall into poverty. Grant me a healthy attitude towards money and break any obsession I may have had with it.

In Jesus' Name,

Amen

# Interaction

Your Prayer:

God's Response:

# 67

## Motives

Psalm 26:2

Proverbs 17:3

# Motives Prayer

Father,

Only you know the heart and you purify it by the tests and trials of life. Thank you for the ways you've been purifying my heart, as hard as it's been; I see how you're using that process to prepare me for the ways you want to use me in ministry. Help me to continue to submit to your refining process and to pray for others who are going through it as well. I can never know their heart and their motives, so help me never to try or make assumptions based on their behavior. As you purify my heart, help me to be motivated by love and to seek to express my love for the people you've brought into my life. The world is so hungry for love and truth and we need more people driven by that truth, love and justice. Help me to be willing to examine my own motives as I relate to others and keep my heart pure before you. Transform my heart and my life for your purpose and help me not to fight against it when it doesn't look the way I thought it would. Help me to trust your process, trust your goodness and believe in the better I will experience with you.

In Jesus' Name,
Amen

# Interaction

Your Prayer:

God's Response:

# 68

# Praise

1 Chronicles 16:25-26

Psalm 92:1

Psalm 86:12

# Praise Prayer

Father,

I praise you because you are worthy. I praise you because you are holy. There is no one like you. There is no one above you. By your word and through your power you made the heavens and the earth. You spoke and set things into motion. I praise you because by your breath, man became a living soul. I praise you because I am fearfully and wonderfully made. I praise you because no one can do what you can do. It is my heart's desire to praise you and when I do I feel your presence and your pleasure. You inhabit the praises of your people, and you tell us to put on the garment of praise for the spirit of heaviness. Praise is powerful and it's a weapon I can use against the enemy. When my circumstances become overwhelming, if I turn my gaze toward you and begin to praise you for who you are, focusing on your character, you become greater in my eyes and my problems become less. Help me to use my voice to sing to you in that midnight hour and watch heaven shake the earth and remove the obstacles that block my path to you. And even when I wake, would you put a melody in my heart that I can sing to you and set my day right. Praising you changes the atmosphere and destroys the darkness. The spirit of oppression cannot survive there. Help me to be quick to lift my praise to you with all my heart and passion and to thank you, giving glory to your name, both now and forever.

In Jesus' Name,

Amen

## Interaction

Your Prayer:

God's Response:

# 69

# Priorities

**Mark 12:29-30**

**Matthew 6:32-34**

# Priorities Prayer

Father,

I ask you to set my priorities right, that you would be the most important part of my existence. I want to love you with a passionate heart, from the depths of my soul, with my every thought and with all my strength. So often the cares of this life get in the way and my striving after success causes me to lose sight of what is important. Forgive me Lord for losing sight of my relationship with you. When I start to drift, gently bring me back to you and remind me that holding onto you is what brings true fulfillment in this life. Help me to constantly seek your kingdom and your righteousness because that is why I'm still here, to bring your kingdom to earth and live rightly before you. When I do this, I become a conduit for your power to flow through me and change the atmosphere. You say that if I seek you, not only will I find you, but I'll be given all other things abundantly. So, help me not to worry about tomorrow, but to deal with each challenge that comes my way, one day at a time. Help me to trust that tomorrow will take care of itself and that you'll be with me then, just as you're faithful to be with me now.

In Jesus' Name,
Amen

## Interaction

Your Prayer:

God's Response:

# 70

## Purity

Psalm 24:3-6

Psalm 86:11

2 Timothy 2:21

# Purity Prayer

Father,

I want my works and ways to be pure, but I struggle in this area. I need your help to choose purity above satisfying my own desires. Make my heart true and sealed by your truth. Show me the way to follow and keep me from deception of any kind. Help me never to deceive others or succumb to deception. Give me eyes to see my way out of the traps of the enemy, so that I remain pure and flee all kind of immorality. "Teach me more about you, how you work and how you move, so that I can walk onward in your truth until everything within me brings honor to your name." Keep me constant in you and make me a pure container of Christ, dedicated to honorable purposes and prepared for every good work you give me to do.

In Jesus' Name,

Amen

# Interaction

Your Prayer:

God's Response:

# 71

## Rest

Matthew 11:28-30

# Rest Prayer

Father,

I'm so tired; tired of fighting, tired of carrying heavy burdens, tired of dealing with the enemy, tired of being afraid to live and love. I need the rest you have to offer me, a rest that I can experience here on this earth, so that I stop longing for death. I long to be with you in eternity because I believe that it's so much better than the things I've been experiencing in this life. There's been so much pain and heartbreak, sometimes I feel like I can't take anymore of it. In those moments, I'm asking that you would come close to me and help me to see you and feel you with me. Heal my broken heart and take the pain away. As I come to you would you refresh me and be the oasis where I can rest in complete safety. As I join my life with yours, help me to walk in step with you and to learn from you how to live and function in this life. Thank you for being so gentle and humble and easy to experience. As I learn how to rest in you, would you break down those walls that I put up to protect myself from getting hurt. That's also part of why I'm so tired. I can't seem to stay connected and out of my fear of getting hurt I pull away from the people who want to love me. Please break me out of that cycle and prepare my heart to experience great love. Help me to be intentional about seeking the rest that you provide that brings me true fulfillment. Help my heart to find rest in you, both now and forever.

In Jesus' Name,

Amen

## Interaction

Your Prayer:

God's Response:

# 72

# Restraint

Proverbs 29:11

Proverbs 25:28

# Restraint Prayer

Father,

I ask that you help me to deal with the feelings of rage that grow inside me when life gets difficult, and I think about the things I've been through. When I experience the judgement of others, it really affects me, and I want to lash out and use a few choice words that I know would not please you because it's not a reflection of you and your love. Help me to exercise restraint in those moments and see what's really going on and why I'm so triggered. I know if I get to the root of my issues, I won't struggle so much with anger, rage, and bitterness. Help me in this area of my life and show me how to live free from the bondages that I have trouble admitting they exist. I can only deal with the things I'm willing to admit are issues and I know you can help me to have the courage to face them and the insight and clarity needed to see the truth and break those chains once and for all. Grant me the fruit of self-control as I spend time in your presence and submit to your process.

In Jesus' Name,

Amen

## Interaction

Your Prayer:

God's Response:

# 73

# Salvation

Exodus 14:13

John 3:16

Psalm 50:23

# Salvation Prayer

Father,

There is so much in your word about salvation and I'm so grateful for the fact that I can turn to your word and receive the guidance and the knowledge I need to help me make it through this life, living for you. Thank you for the gift of salvation that comes by believing in your Son, Jesus Christ. You gave your son to die for our sins, because you loved the world, and now belief in him gives us eternal life. I am so grateful for your sacrifice and for making a way for me to be in relationship with you and enjoy you for all eternity. Lord, I'm also grateful for the word that I hold onto today that tells me to stand still and watch you rescue me, because the enemy I see today I will never see again. There is so much power in those words, and I believe that when I hold onto those words, I experience your salvation in my circumstances. And Lord, I desperately need your salvation, because the devil is real, and his tactics are serious and make life overwhelming for me at times. But I know from your word that when I live a life that pleases you, living in the gratitude of grace, always choosing to walk with you in what is right; this sacrifice leads to more of your salvation and that is what I desire. Save me even from myself, when I'm struggling and considering engaging in behavior that does not please you. Keep me from self-sabotage and instead help me to continue walking with you on the path that leads to life, love, joy, peace and hope today.

In Jesus' Name,

Amen

## Interaction

Your Prayer:

God's Response:

# 74

# Thankfulness

Psalm 9:1

Colossians 3:15

Colossians 2:7

# Thankfulness Prayer

Father,

I can't express enough how thankful I am for all you have done for me. You've changed me and given me a new life. I never want to stop saying thank you. I want to tell everyone I know how good you've been to me and acknowledge all the things you've seen me through. I could not have made it without you. Let my heart be guided by your peace and cause me to always be thankful, even in the dark times. Let me find my way to your light and follow the path that leads to your presence. May I always be grateful for your presence and never treat you as common. Cause my spiritual roots to go deeply into you and continue to fill me with your strength and encouragement. As I sit in your presence, may I absorb your faith and be enriched by my devotion to you. Lord, I choose to keep an attitude of thankfulness and identify the ways you have been faithful to me, so that I don't lose hope when things become challenging. I will remember your goodness and thank you for your patience with me and for the ways you are already at work, even when I can't see it. When I remain thankful, I tap into the channel of your grace, and I receive just what you know I need in that moment. I bless you for this and for your continued influence on my life.

In Jesus' Name,

Amen

# Interaction

Your Prayer:

God's Response:

# 75

# Wisdom

James 1:5

# Wisdom Prayer

Father,

I need your wisdom in my life. I get so lost in my problems that I forget that you're right here, ready to guide me and show me what to do. All I have to do is ask. So today I'm asking. Lord, would you grant me the wisdom to know how to handle the challenges in my life that have developed because of the things I've never been exposed to. I find myself naïve and not always able to handle difficult situations and it leads me to want to give up the fight. Help me when I struggle to keep my will to live. Help me when I've lost all perspective and death seems more attractive to me than living. I need your wisdom in these moments and I need your grace to help me in my weakness. Show me how to walk out of the darkness and into your light. Let your love envelop me when I'm feeling like I have no good way out of my current circumstances and show me the way to a better life with you. I want to make good, wise choices that are based on my understanding of who you are in my life and the reality that I can face any challenge with you holding my hand and guiding me. It's you and me Lord, walking together, loving each other. That is what I want, and I believe that in this desire is the greatest wisdom. Help me to walk in it always and to never lose sight of who you are to me. You are my heart, you are my life, you are my everything. Thank you for being my all in all.

In Jesus' Name,
Amen


**Interaction**


Your Prayer:


God's Response:

# 76

# Words

## Proverbs 18:21

# Words Prayer

Father,

I realize that words have great power to create life like you did when you spoke the world into existence, but they also how the power to kill and destroy like Jesus did when he cursed the fig tree and it withered up from the root. I know that I'm made in your image and as your daughter, I have been given the power to give life or to kill with my words and I don't ever want to take that power lightly. Help me to be careful with my words, to think before I speak and to choose to speak words that build people up instead of tearing them down. Help me to be mindful of the words I speak about myself as well. Help me not to belittle myself or speak words of negativity that kill my dreams before they ever have a chance to blossom. I want my words to matter, and I want to speak words to you that show how much I love you and tell of how grateful I am for how you saved my life. Let loving, beautiful words flow from my lips on a regular basis and may I reap the rewards of releasing love and kindness into the atmosphere. Thank you for the power you have given me to speak life over my circumstances and to see growth happen inside my heart. Transform me by the power of your Holy Spirit and let me walk along the path you have cleared for me.

In Jesus' Name,

Amen

**Interaction:**

Your Prayer:

God's Response:

# 77

# Worship

Psalm 145:3

Psalm 5:7

Romans 12:1

# Worship Prayer

Father,

You are amazing! I am in awe of how wonderful and great you are. You are always worthy of my praise and worship. I get excited any time I come into your presence to worship you in your house. There's something so powerful about corporate worship and I feel like in those moments all of heaven is worshipping with us and you hear it all. When I worship you in private, I get the sense that it pleases you even more because there's no distraction, just me expressing my heart to you, telling you through song how much you mean to me. It's in worship that I feel your pleasure and that blesses my heart and my life. Lord, I know that worship is not just about singing praises to you, but it's about surrendering myself to you, to be a living sacrifice. It's not easy to make sacrifices for you, but you did it for me in the greatest way, so my heart's response is naturally to be willing to make sacrifices for you. It's a sacrifice to live a holy life, but I know that's what pleases your heart and that's what I want more than anything, to please you and live my life in such a way that demonstrates how much I love you. I am so grateful for you today. You've saved my life and changed me in ways I had no right to expect. I love you and I bless your name today. Keep my heart tender before you, so that I'm quick to worship you when it feels like my life is falling apart. When I reach those hard moments, let my worship bring your presence and change the atmosphere, so that I can weather the storm with you and come out the other side stronger, more whole and full of your power to do your will.

In Jesus' Name,

Amen

# Interaction

Your Prayer:

God's Response:

 Loretta Fralin-Rapp is a writer with a passion to see others find a meaningful walk with God. She is the author of *Confessions for the Narrow Road: It's Within You*, which is 40-day devotional that focuses on the power of choices and making confessions that can change the course of one's life. In her own walk with God, she's had to battle living with bipolar disorder and learning how to depend on Him to sustain her during the dark days of depression and the highs of mania that led to her becoming separated from her daughter going on 12 years. It's been a challenging experience, one that has brought her close to God and as she shares her journey in *Confessions for the Narrow Road: It's Within You*, she encourages others to choose life.

She is currently attending Denver Seminary in Colorado and seeks to receive her master's in divinity with a concentration in chaplaincy to work as a Prison Chaplain. It is her desire to work with the incarcerated who suffer with mental illness and eventually help those who are released from prison find mental health recovery.

Loretta is passionate about the word of God and prayer and enjoys reading nonfiction. She also enjoys walking in the beautiful place that is Colorado and she is happy to call it home.

Printed in the USA
CPSIA information can be obtained
at www.ICGtesting.com
CBHW070403190724
11674CB00019B/903